Library of Congress Cataloging-in-Publication Data

Dedicated to the two mothers in my life and my wife: Glenda Urmacher

In Memory of
My Mother Chaya Appelbaum-Urmacher
My Mother-in-law Adele Britvan-Eiss
My Aunt Eva Urmacher-Sklarsky
"who helped with my story"
My Immediate Family who perished in the Holocaust

Table of Contents

-

Chapter 1 – prologue

Many years have passed but the memories of the war are so clear and so deeply ingrained in my being that I am able to relive every moment as if it were yesterday. It was as if living an unexplained nightmare; there were countless moments of tremendous horror. These memories follow me everywhere, whether I want them to or not. They do not ask me for permission. They just invade my personal space.

My story does not claim to be a factual account of events but of my personal experiences and imprinted memories.

In 1981, I was working in the aerospace industry as a senior engineer. As a computer analyst, I supported Space Shuttle 1 "Columbia" at the Kennedy Space Center. Often the control center was dark only illuminated by the endless panels of red blinking lights. My mind sometimes wandered to another time and place. It is Poland, 1939. World War II came quickly and painfully when German Luftwaffe planes bombed Poland. I was left with an indelible reminder, a scar on my left thigh.

Chapter 2 - Poland

I was born the town of Siedlce (pronounced "shed-lit-see"), Poland, which is in the eastern part of the country. The area later became infamous due to its proximity to the Nazi death camp of Treblinka.

A vibrant secular middle and upper class Jewish community comprised half of Siedlce's 30,000 inhabitants. That is until the city was occupied by German troops on September 1, 1939. I was 4 years old.

The head of my family was my father who was one of the Zionist Haluzim or Israeli pioneers. The Zionist Haluzim helped to drain the swamps of Palestine in the 1920s. My father, Samuel Urmacher was a photographer by profession.

My mother Chaya came from an observant Jewish family and was a "balabusta," a homemaker. I also had a younger sister, Ruth.

My paternal and maternal grandparents lived in nearby Biala-Podlaska, Poland, along with numerous other aunts, uncles, and cousins. Both sides of our collective families had known each other and had lived in this part of Poland for generations.

My Urmacher Polish family in a photo dated 1920. From left to right in the front row are Grandmother, Aunt Eva, and Grandfather. Behind Grandfather is my oldest Aunt Cippora, who went to Palestine with my father but stayed there while my father returned to Poland. On the far right is my father, along with other aunts and uncles. Note the polish military uniforms of the young men. They served in the Polish army that later collaborated with the German Nazis.

Most of my family perished in the Holocaust, except for my father, some of my mother's family, my sister & me.

Prior to the war, we had lived fairly comfortable middle class lives. My father's photo /optic store was located on the 1st floor of a building that was owned by my paternal grandfather. Our family lived above the store, as was the custom for many city dwellers. We had a large attic that was my playroom and I remember a toy airplane that hung from the rafters. It was so huge and it was all mine.

At the beginning of Shabbat and the Jewish holidays, we visited and dined with my grandparents along with other family members and neighbors who were both Jewish and non-Jewish. The meals were long and elaborate. As I look back, I am amazed at the production that went on every week without the modern conveniences that we now have. Though my grandmother was very tiny, she produced an elaborate and wonderful "erev Shabbat." The silver was polished until it shone, and everything was gleaming white, from the linens, to the china, to the serving platters.

My grandfather, who was stern and proud, sat at head of the table wrapped in his prayer tallit. Even as a young child, I realized that this Shabbat dinner was very special, and I knew I had to be on my best behavior.

My grandfather, professor at the Warsaw University, also owned the first movie theater in our town. I remember being terrified of the first war movie I ever saw.

My grandfather holding me in front my father's store.

My childhood memories are few before the war. Those that I have are filled with remembrances of free time to play with friends in the local parks and being surrounded by family and friends who loved and cared for me.

In the picture taken in 1937, I am the smiling child in the middle.

Chapter 3 – War 1939

After the invasion of Poland by Germany, and the subsequent agreement between Hitler and Stalin, under the terms of the Nazi-Soviet Pact, Poland was divided into two states: one belonging to Germany and the other belonging to the Soviet Union. The rivers Pisa, Narew, Bug and San became the borderline between the two states.

28 September 1939

On Saturday, the second day of the war, the bombing of Siedlce began. My father left to find gas masks and my mother, sister and I were in the courtyard of our apartment. I heard airplanes overhead and the bombs started to fall from the sky like red balls of fire. Even now if I close my eyes, I can see a red stone dropping from the plane like a red brick. Suddenly there was silence and my family was buried in rubble. We were dug out of the rubble by our neighbors. I had been injured by a piece of shrapnel in my left thigh and was bleeding. Luckily my mother and sister were not hurt. We began looking for shelter, and started to walk the street. The town was on fire, my mother was holding my hand, and caring my sister. I was in bleeding and in shock.

My father returned to find a demolished building where our home and family business had been. A neighbor told him we were in the courtyard when the bombing started. He found my shoe and my mother's shawl and he thought we were dead. Three days later a friend saw him wandering around town stunned and in shock. The neighbor asked him where he had been because his wife and children were looking for him, and were afraid he had died in the bombing. The neighbor told him that we were taken to the market square. We were reunited in the Market Square with rest of Jewish town population.

The Germans bombed Siedlce for days and days. Many towns people that weren't buried alive in the rubble, jumped out of the windows of burning buildings. Tragically the buildings bombed were not military installations since there were none in our town, but schools, hospitals, grain warehouses and railroad tracks. The town was on fire. The streets were covered with rubble from the buildings and dismembered parts of bodies. Panic broke out. Polish men, women and children, non-Jews and former neighbors and friends, would run ahead of the Germans, pointing out the Jewish homes and stores. The Nazis then began arresting Jews, and marched us all, old and young, to the Market Square. We were reunited in Market Square and in tears.

Horse drawn buggy

We managed to escape the Market
Square and find a horse and buggy we
loaded our possessions onto the cart.
My sister and I were put on top of the
cart and so we started our journey to
my Aunt Eva's family farm in Stolin,
Belarus where we thought we would
be safe. The road was littered with
broken down cars and carts, dead
horses and other animals. I was crying
and my mother covered my sister and
me with a blanket.

German planes were strafing us, so
we hid in the forest by day and walked

the road at night. We were stopped often by German and Polish authorities that my father bribed with gold coins hidden in our clothing. But when he ran out of gold coins, we were arrested and all of our possessions were taken. The German/Polish army commandeered our cart and horse and they immediately closed in on us with snapping, growling dogs that looked as if they would tear us apart.

The Germans marched us to a train stop, which was essentially a camp, since it was ringed by a fence, and where families with kids like us, were guarded by large and vicious dogs.

The Germans stood by a wire fence, and encouraged dogs to intimidate us. The sick and elderly were shot, and any hole could become their instant grave. The Germans shot anybody that began to look sick. I was terrified and crying and for the Germans that was entertainment. During all this time, the bombing continued to explode all around us. If the country is already occupied, there is no bombing because they might hit their own soldiers.

One night, during heavy bombing, we managed to escape. We were still trying to reach Aunt Eva's farm but since we had heard that the Germans were guarding the main roads and beating all Jews, we traveled by back roads... Again we hid in the forest by day and walked only at night.

We stayed with my Aunt Eva's family relative who had a nearby farm. The farm was on the Russian side Because of Poland's "Stalin/Hitler" division; the farm was on the Russian side we were safe from the Germans. I was reunited with my cousin Yurek who was two years older than me. He was my best friend.

But we were not allowed to live in peace, The Russian authorities told us we must become citizens and join the communist party. My father refused because we planned to join my father's sister in Palestine. Because my family refused to become communist party members, secret political police called NKVD invaded our house at 2 am and began harassing us. They then told us that we were being sent to a labor camp. Yurek and I were scared and hysterical. Our parents were given only 15 minutes to secure some food and warm clothing.

The truck driver and Russian soldiers began to push us onto the truck. We arrived at a train depot that was already packed with thousands of people and their belongings. The soldiers were shouting for us to board a very long train of cattle cars. (Between 1939-1941, 300,000 Jews escaped to Russia but some wound up at labor camps "gulags")

Chapter 4 – The Train/cattle cars

I can still remember that my cousin Yurek and I were crying hysterically and were extremely frightened. The soldiers were shouting at everyone to get on the train.

Finally the doors were closed and locked. The train left picking up speed. Yurek and I were frantically looking for a hole or space in the wall so that we could look outside but the older kids kept pushing us away.

The heat and the smell were unbearable. There were no restrooms so someone made a hole in the floor and that served as a toilet without walls.

I found a hole that I could breathe out of and fell asleep listening to the sound of the train tracks "ta-ta...ta-ta...ta-ta".

Every once in a while the train stopped briefly and we were given some water and bread. Soon lice infected us and it became my mother's daily activity was to try to remove as many lice from our heads as possible WE were told not to scratch, but the itching was constant. Yurek and I fought with other kids to be by a window but there was only enough space for two kids and the older kids were stronger than us. We were on the train for days.

Finally the train stopped by a river and we were told to get off. My mother held my hand as we got into the river and washed the lice off our bodies. The children were all told to get into a boat to cross the river while the adults waded through the water. Yurek, my sister and I were crying because we were alone while my mother and father walked across the river. At night we were all ordered to regroup and start walking. It was very bright and there were huge mosquitoes that bit us. We finally arrived in a deserted place in the forest where we were told we were now Stalin's slaves and this place would be our home forever.

Chapter 5 – Siberia (gulag)

After a thirty-kilometer march through the forest we arrived in the middle of a clearing with a big bunkhouse. The Major of the labor camp introduced himself and announced we would be his slaves. All 300 of us were going to be placed in the bunkhouse but there weren't any beds, tables or even a chair. The Major said that in the forest around us there was a lot of good wood and we should be able to build beds, chairs and a table. We slept on the floor and they gave us three meals a day but there wasn't any meat, fruit or vegetables. Bread and potatoes or soup my mother was an Observant Jew and kept kosher. Someone was able to kill a bear for food but my mother wouldn't eat it because it wasn't kosher.

She found a rabbi who taught me what it meant to be a Jew. I remember his long white beard and sitting beside him while he taught me "the shema" and morning prayers. Everyone had to work including the women and the elderly. My aunt Eva took care of Yurek, my sister and me. She took us for walks in forest and we would gather berries to eat. And mushrooms

In Siberia, my father worked as a laborer cutting ice blocks, which were then used to build roads. My father, mother and my uncle used to walk in the forest every night. We made and maintained the ice block roads which were used for transporting the timber from the forest in subzero temperatures. My aunt Eva told the Russian soldiers that my father and uncle knew how to make optic lenses and had experience with cameras and photography.

The commander of the camp had a picture of his family that my father and uncle enlarged using chemicals and a piece of glass. When they were able to prove their skill, the commander made them work as photographers for the military.

I was 7 years old when my mother died of cholera July of 1942.

My mother with my sister

This photo was given to me four years ago by a family member, and is the only picture that I have of my mother. Prior to four years ago, for more than 60 years, my mother was a faceless image that haunted me nightly. I still cannot connect this picture and my mother's face. The only memory I have of my mother is of her in a darkened hut with her hand out telling me not to come near her because cholera was contagious. Her job in the camp was to help nurse the sick and elderly.

After she died, I was all alone with no one to comfort or take care of me. The rabbi, who was teaching me schema, told me that my mother was in heaven with G-d and that He was with me. I survived my time alone only because I knew that G-d was always with me.

In 1942, Stalin authorized Polish soldiers to go to either the Middle East or China where they could be trained by the British to start another front with the Germans. My family "Urmacher, Sklarsky" wanted to go with them. We went from Siberia to Uzbekistan and Tashkent on our way to China. In Tashkent we left the train and I remember my family stayed in one room in Tashkent. My father met a woman who "agreed" to take care of my sister and me.

I remember she gave us a piece of bread with butter on it. Later she got in a fight with my sister and our father threw my sister and me out of the house. In Tashkent my father opened a photography store.

Chapter 6 – 1945 Back in Poland

I am in Poland alone with some friends on the bombed streets.

A few years later, after the end of World War II, there was a train going back to Poland with a lot of Jews and we went with them. We were part of several hundred survivors who tried to make our way back to our homes in

Poland. The trains were being stopped by Polish citizens who didn't want the Jewish population returning to their homes, businesses, and farms the Polish had confiscated, and the Polish had made their own.

Survivors of Nazi concentration camps and the Russian gulags in Siberia; emaciated men, women and children, pathetic remnants of humanity were pulled off trains and slaughtered by their Polish neighbors. We survived only because my father and some other men grabbed an ax and threatened to kill the conductor of the train if he didn't keep the train moving.

I heard people praying the Schema. On the trains as we were being attacked because that is the prayer Jews say when they are about to die. Now every time I hear the

Shema, I automatically think of those trains and hearing all of those people praying and the unspeakable massacre.

Start of the orphanage in Poland with a guard

The woman my father was with now refused to take care of us so my sister and I were sent to an improvised orphanage where we were cared for by the survivors and Jewish partisans of the Warsaw Ghetto. The partisans served in the Polish army and some were officers that my father had served with.

We were cared for in the orphanage by ghetto survivors and partisans.

To stay alive we were constantly moved or hidden in the forest. It was imperative that we needed to be quiet so some of us were drugged so we would not make noise.

The Polish people continually attacked the orphanage so we were given a guard. There was limited amount of food but in order for us to get food from the nuns we needed to cross ourselves even though the food was from the US Army. The partisans showed us how to make a razor blade crystal radio.

Chapter 7 Rosenheim, Germany

Displaced Persons Camp (DP)

The orphanage in Rosenheim,
Germany

The goal of the orphanage was to find all the surviving Jewish orphans in Poland keep them alive and transport them to Israel Palestine (which was still under British control) at any and all costs. The orphanage grew in size, as more children were found alive without their families.

At the orphanage we were taught only Hebrew and that Israel would be our sanctuary. The orphanage sent us from Poland to Rosenheim, Germany, Rosenheim to a displaced persons camp (DP Camp "United Nations Relief and Rehabilitation Administration (UNRRA)

The US Army (UNRRA) took care of all the food and essentials. This was the first time I drank Carnation milk and I was sick with boils all over my body. ORT (was founded in Tsarist Russia in 1880, is a Russian acronym) started an educational program sponsored by American Jewish Relief.

My father arrived with his new wife and she was pregnant. He was friendly with the American army personnel.

Chapter 8 – Exodus 1947

The orphanage staff chose some children to be the first group to reach Israel. My sister and I were happy to have been picked,

קבוצה
דרור
מרוזנהים

בדרך לעליה

1947 II 24

I am bottom left, my sister top left

US Army trucks picked us up for the start of the journey. In the group photo below, my father is saying good-bye to us.

We traveled to the French border but we needed to sneak into France without the British becoming aware that the final destination was Palestine (Israel). We crossed from English sector to the Frenche sector by foot. In France we were like tourists.

We proceeded to board the ship
"Exodus 47" at Port of Sate near
Marseilles. Were you the only group
or were there orphans from other
displaced person's camp. We were
jammed together on sleeping cots
with no privacy. As soon as we set
sail, the British war ships were on us.

The British frigates were tailing us.
We were given cooked meals and
water. We washed using salt water on
the ship that was organized and run
by the Haganah, a Jewish paramilitary

organization. (Years later I met the woman who worked with the Haganah on the Exodus.) During the journey we were told how to prepare for the British interception.

Can't throw a potato more than 20-30 feet so why bother?

The British boarded the ship after a weeklong journey. There was a fight and we threw potatoes and oranges while the British used guns and tear gas. They shot a boy from my orphanage and killed an American volunteer. I was 12 years old and was told to stay below the deck. I was frightened because I heard the screams and could smell the tear gas and the gunpowder.

The British frigates were playing ping-pong, using our ship as a net. They hit us from both sides. The ship's hull started to break up and I wound up in the water but did not know how to swim.

The British ship towed the crippled ship to Haifa.

We were transferred to three cargo ships. Which were ordered to return us to France, We were placed in "ship's cargo bay".

We were very crowded and had to sleep on the floor. Soon we arrived at a port near Marseilles, France. I remember looking down to the pier. Two women were looking up at us. One was wearing a US army uniform and the other woman was a civilian.

In 1998, in Los Angeles, I met Ruth Gruber the author of "EXODUS 1947".

Ruth Gruber was the woman in the US Army uniform. She interviewed me for a book she was writing, "EXODUS 1947". (At the interview I was told that the civilian woman was in the Haganah said that now the United Nations would vote for petition Palestine to the nation Israel).

Chapter 9 – Germany (Hamburg)

The orphanage did not disembark. The ship left France and we sailed to Hamburg, Germany. We were in the English Channel and the water was very rough with big waves. We arrived at Hamburg and were placed in a prison camp with barbed wire and German guards. The camp smelled of gunpowder and I thought I was back where I started.

But all was not lost. A new ship was found and again we were smuggled and some of us were drugged to be quiet as we boarded a ship for Israel.

Again I was drugged and smuggled from Hamburg, Germany to Israel.

Chapter 10- Israel

I was a wreck when I arrived in Israel, which was still British mandate of Palestine. I stuttered and was withdrawn. The orphanage stayed in a rehab center and I finally learned how to swim there.

Then I went to my aunt Cippora who had stayed in Israel when my father went back to Poland. I met my father and told him I want to be with him and be a family again, but his wife didn't want us. I was crying but it was no use. My aunt wanted my sister and me to stay with her but that wasn't an option. I went to one kibbutz and my sister to another. And we were abandoned again and separated.

Somehow, as sometimes happens in life, the kibbutz was the best thing for me. In the kibbutz I worked in the machine shop and read every technical book I could find. I learned English, studied math, chemistry and physics. I fixed the radios for the kibbutz and operated the movie projector when we watched movies. I performed experiments building solar energy cell in a jar.

The members of this kibbutz were mostly from United States. They taught me and supplied me with all the books I needed. They asked me to build a perpetual motion machine. It took me a year to figure out that it was not possible because energy is constantly changing.

Before joining the Israeli army in 1952, I went to Jerusalem to study religion for two weeks. I was 17 and a half when I went into the army while everyone around me was already 18.

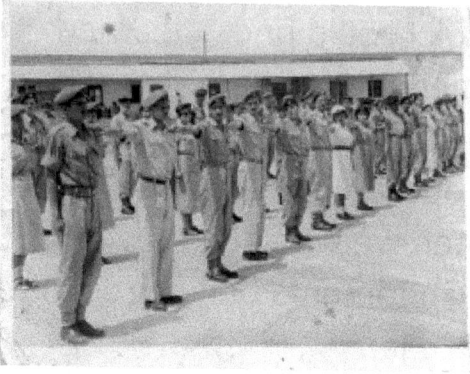

In the army, I was given an aptitude test. Since I scored high, I was sent to school to become a medic. Even though I cannot stand the sight of blood, I treated two cases, a bullet wound in a leg and a stomach wound. I took the injured to the field hospital in a truck.

Part of our training was learning history by hiking to the sites of wars and kings' victories described in the bible I served in the army for two years.

Going back to the kibbutz life and farming was not for me and by now engineering was in my blood. I worked in a machine shop fixing tractors and farm equipment.

Not having a home or even a room to go to, I decided to work on a ship as machinist. I took courses at the Haifa Teknion to get a better understanding of this profession, My cousin, Yakov Ritov, was a captain in the navy and he helped me get my first job as a machinist on Zim Shipping. Line. When the ships were at sea and a part of an engine had to be replaced, that part had to be made on the ship. I was very surprised that I could make parts using the machine shop.

I worked on five ships that were either steam or diesel. I sailed the Mediterranean Sea, Pacific and Atlantic Oceans as well as the Red Sea and I sailed in all kinds of bad weather. I picked up a new ship in Hamburg, Germany. I danced with a girl who asked me if I was Jewish or Israeli. I told her I was Jewish and an Israeli.

Year 1960 I was working on the SS Jerusalem. During the winter we sailed from New York to the

Caribbean. On the SS Jerusalem, I was promoted to an Engineering Officer.

On one of the trips, I met a beautiful and smart woman and I was impressed with the way she held herself. Right then I asked her for a date. She said she loved my uniform.

After of couple of dates with Glenda, I asked her to marry me. Glenda was going to school and working in New York and was living on Long Island.

Glenda took me to meet her parents on Long Island. I was enchanted and proposed we discussed where we would live. I preferred Israel but the big problem was my working on the ship and long separations. Glenda was very close with her family and her family was in New York. We decided to get married in Israel and I sent Glenda air tickets to Tel Aviv. The first problem was that we needed to prove that Glenda is Jewish. This problem was solved when we discovered we are related by marriage through cousins in Argentina. We got married in Tel Aviv's Dan Hotel in June 1961.

Chapter 11- USA

Photographed on board.RMS. QUEEN MARY.

Honeymoon onboard the Queen Mary 1

I immigrated to the US on a Polish quota as the Israel quota had been filled for the year I needed it. October 1961 we arrived in New York City on the original Queen Mary 1, rented a vacant apartment in the Kew Gardens area of Queens.

We saved enough money, living free of charge with Glenda's parents on Long Island, for a month's rent and

security deposit, with enough left over for a box spring and mattress.
Glenda's aunt Gloria lent us her bridge table and four chairs.

I needed to reeducate. I was hired by a ship building company and they were building a brand new hydrofoil for the military. They brought me in because I had a license from an international engineering company from my days on the ship. After four days they escorted me to the gate because they realized I wasn't a citizen and that project was top secret.

My first job was with Long Island Railroad as a machinist. At night I was going to computer programing school. Then I went to ESSO gas station management school. I opened an ESSO station on a busy corner. Our daughter was born.

Mother- in- law Adele loaned us down payment for a house. I was working long hours at the station fixing cars and selling gas. We sold the station, and I started a new company American Electronic. I fixed televisions, radios and refrigerators. I enrolled in Farmingdale University studying computer programing. Between the businesses and the university I was still working long hours. I received my U.S. citizenship on November 4, 1965.

I continued with the university and got a job in OGDAN testing hardware that was used by NASA for the moon shot. Glenda was driving me between the job and university with a sandwich for lunch or supper.

There was an opening with Honeywell for a computer hardware/software engineer and I applied. I was given an aptitude test and I was hired.

I was working in Manhattan NY and driving from Long Island. I was on call to fix hardware/software.

Ten engineers were chosen from all the states for the new computer product line and I was one of them. I spend six months in Newton, MA designing the new operating system. I drove home every weekend to Long Island.

Then, still with Honeywell, we moved to California.

Honeywell decided they were going to build a new computer design. In France that was based on Multex, a super secure operating system. Ten engineers went to Paris. Again I was chosen and I brought my wife and 2 daughters. We rented an apartment near the Eiffel Tower and spent 11 months in Paris.

We returned to Los Angeles and I continued to work at Honeywell while attending school at California Western University and UCLA. In 1975 I wrote my dissertation on computer security privacy. I had to convince my graduate advisor that this topic would be important in the future.

I graduated with a MBA. In 1979 I was hired by Aerospace as Senior Engineering Specialist, and I worked on numerous projects.

In 1995 I envisioned that the year 2000 could be a problem for the computer industry. I retired and wrote a program to analyze computer languages to determine whether there would be problems in 2000. I formed a company called Computer Performance Engineering solely for the year 2000 problem. I retired and am living in Southern California. We visit Israel almost every other year. On one of the visits at my sister's house, my cousin Yaakov who has Alzheimer's disease asked me when I was coming home to Israel.

I received company awards from Honeywell and Aerospace.

I never talked about my background to any of my coworkers. I have bad nightmares. In my work travels, alone in hotels, I would study/review my work materials till I was exhausted and then would fall asleep.

To this day, I continue to have bad nightmares.

Chapter 12- Epilogue

In the end I won the war. I moved to America and I have my family. My wife Glenda, my daughters Carrie and Bridget, my son- in- law Scott Sommer and my grandchildren Colin, Dylan and Drew.

Sources and Acknowledgments

Photos are from family collection.

1998 I was interviewed by "SURVIVORS OF THE SHOAH Visual History Foundation.

1998 I was interviewed by Ruth Gruber for the book "the ship that launched a nation" EXODUS 1947.

PERMISSION FORM

DATE: November 19.2012

NAME: Rhea Carmi

ADDRESS: 18945 Kirkcolm Lane, Porter Ranch, CA 91326

E-mail: rhea@carmi.us

Dear Rhea Carmi,

Uri Urmacher is preparing to published a book

Pub. Date:	2012-2013	Print run	TBA
Cover:	Hard & Soft	Price:	TBA
Pages:	TBA	Market:	World wide

May Uri Urmacher have non-exclusive rights to use the following material in this book and in future printings and editions . If you do not control these rights in their entirety kindly let me know whom else I must contact.

Requested material:

Selection: DESCRIBE THE MATERIAL i.e. PAGE NUMBER OR SUBTITLE
            DESCRIPTION OF IMAGE (include dimensions and medium):

Source: TITLE OF PUBLICATION OR IMAGE : HUMANITIY'S STRUGGLES LXXIII , 1979

Author: AUTHOR OF MATERIAL Rhea Carmi

We will use the following credit line unless otherwise indicated:

From TITLE by AUTHOR Copyright © YEAR by COPYRIGHTHOLDER Reprinted by permission.

I grant permission for the use requested above:

Rhea Carmi November 19.2012

Signature:

Sabbath Dinner and Screening
Hillel at Chapman University is Proud
to announce the screening of·
Exodus 1947
The Ship that Launched a Nation
Written Produced & Directed by
Elizabeth Rodgers & Robby Henson
Narrated by Morley Safer
Friday February 18", 2011
6:00 pm
Chaplain University
Fish Interfaith center
I University Drive
Orange", 92866
Featuring Q& A with Holocaust
Survivor and Exodus 1947
12 year old refugee
Uri Urmacher
Hillel CHAPMAN UNIVERSITY
Event Sponsored by Chapman Hillel

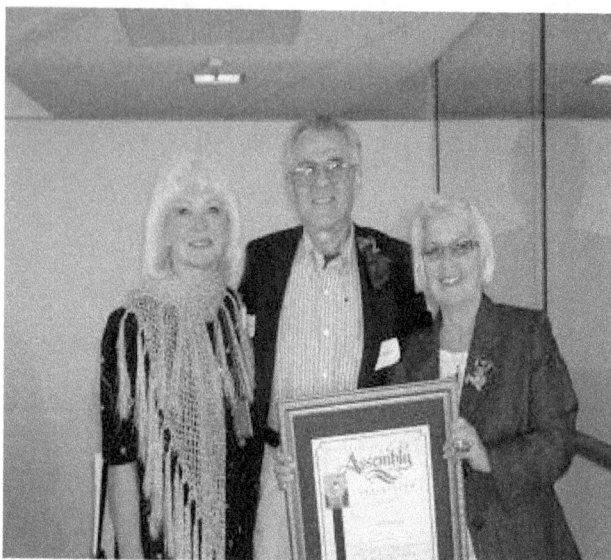

Holocaust Memorial Project
local reception 2010 by
Assemblywomen Bonnie Lowenthal